praise for *"of the angels"*

"At a time when so many neighborhoods are slowly being gentrified and L.A. natives are being displaced, *of the angels* helps to canonize what it's really like to grow up in Los Angeles as a first generation Latina, descended from immigrants. Alejandra Medina makes my city beautiful, by taking us on a tour of MacArthur Park, Angelino Heights, Olvera Street, the Downtown L.A. of old and so much more. This is the type of book I've always wanted to read: one that casts the city as both protagonist and the backdrop on which folks do their living."

— **Maricella Aldana,** Los Angeles native

"Alejandra Medina's debut poetry chapbook *of the angels* is a personal, moving tribute to our shared city of Los Angeles. So often misunderstood, mischaracterized, diminished, white-washed, this "ghostly world hidden in smog" becomes love songs, bus rides, poppy blooms, the twenty-sixth floor of city hall, and much more in Medina's hands. Through her gorgeous language, she unspools cliché, crosses geographic and linguistic borders, and creates a new myth of home, family, community, and love. When you have no say in where you were born and raised, is it circumstance that keeps us here? she asks. Or is it the people? The memories? The place itself? For all Angelenos, this is a must-read. For everyone, this is an L.A. you haven't seen immortalized on the page before."

— **Sofía Aguilar**, author of *amor.* and *STREAMING SERVICE: the series finale*

"Romantic, warm, comforting as your favorite cup of tea, and unique all the same. In *of the angels*, Alejandra Medina's voice is reminiscent of a Mary Oliver in Los Angeles, while maintaining a fresh perspective from someone who's truly in love with the city. This is the type of writer—and collection —that poetry needs today: something rooted in tradition, honest to a fault, and entirely new. Medina does not only remember where she came from; she pays a stunning homage to it."

— **Paula Macenas**, author of *when the world ends this time*

"Alejandra Medina's chapbook, *of the angels,* is an exquisite body of work. Her pieces focus on Los Angeles, honoring culture, history, family, love, and so much more. Her writing technique throughout the collection is brilliant, from word choice to form to storytelling. She brings the readers into the scope and heart of Los Angeles by sharing personal narratives and the Latine/x experience. Alejandra is an Ambassador for my program, and I'm so proud of their work! She inspires her colleagues from the program with her clever style and technique. We love her cheerful attitude, and I can't wait for you all to read this chapbook!"

— **Celeste Alyssa Gomez**, author & founder of La Poeta Publications

"In *of the angels*, Alejandra Medina writes about the place-deep love we've been missing, not merely as a polished promise of throwbacks crooning from lowriders, but something truer: love that hopes to root itself in concrete and bloom anyway. These poems breathe in the essence of Los Angeles envisioning palm trees like upside-down brooms sweeping up the moon, while downtown streets are folded into the lifelines of a palm. The city becomes a sanctuary shaped by its people and their words. Medina's work understands what it means to be caught between the land before and the pavement now. Her lines trace ancestry through the curve of a jaw, and you can taste the words breaking on the tongue as if the speaker is finding their voice through you. This collection will make you feel as the night does—held close, something you want to rest in for a while. With the wisdom that the bluest love means embracing a city's dark and hidden complexity, these poems are visceral and loud as trompetas. And to borrow from "oldiez": pure as an... [East LA summer sky]."

— **Shandela Contreras**,
award-winning spoken-word poet & author of *Every Beautiful Pen Bleeds Through*

"Los Angeles is often the misunderstood daughter of the West Coast, many not being able to pierce its inner soul beyond the city's obvious glitz and glamour. *of the angels* captures the essence of this perfectly imperfect city: its soul, its people, and the stories of the unseen and underepresented that have built it from the ground up. Alejandra portrays this city with the sincere tenderness, affection, and honesty it deserves: through the eyes of a true Los Angeles native. This poetess paints a picture of the city inspired by her love for her community, dripping in dignity and humble adoration."

— **Joan Abigail Mabansag**
Editor & Graphic Design Lead, La Poeta Publications

of the angels

poems

Alejandra Medina

Cover Design & Interior Formatting
by Joan Abigail Mabansag

Printed in the United States of America

First Printing, 2026
ISBN 979-8-9869099-4-3
La Poeta Publications
www.LaPoetaPublications.com

contents

letter from the author 11

amtrak 13
chicano yearn 15
santa desconocida 19
the american dreamer awakens 21
my father teaches me to whistle 24
middle 25
our neighborhood's gone bad 26
somewhere on mulholland drive 27
my situationship thinks he's better than me 29
tectonic 31
malibu, ca 32
no. 61 34
mnemonic 37
city hall, 26th floor 38
palm 40
la llorona at the border 42
the flower vendor 43
no sabo[1] 44
you hate L.A. traffic 46
late night drive home 48
a rorschach on the moon 50
angeleno sunsets remind me of you 52
ghazal for westlake/macarthur park 53
las viejitas on the metro a-line want to be immortal 55
oldiez 58
we walk through angelino heights 59
what i know about "el lay" 61
homecoming 65

notes 67
acknowledgements 69
about the author 71

Dear Reader,

The land we know as the Los Angeles Basin exists atop Tovangar, the ancestral land of the Gabrielino-Tongva tribe. I would like to acknowledge them as the first true Angelenos. To learn more about their history, culture, and current impact, you can visit their page: gabrielinotongva.org.

***

This poetry collection is about the Los Angeles I grew up in. In other words, it is about a predominantly Hispanic and Latino city of immigrants, written in Spanglish. If you are looking to read about celebrities, Hollywood, the film making industry or anything of the sort, you will not find it here. But stay awhile anyway and learn to look at the city from a different perspective: one that is not white-washed and gentrified but rich in culture and rooted in history.

Con mucho amor,
Alejandra Medina

amtrak

take me upstate, up to san francisco
on the amtrak. straight through california
farmland: bakersfield, fresno, stockton. grass
yellowing in the heat, the earth yielding

to the crop. let me gaze upon all these
mountains along the highway, imagine
myself rooted deep within them like i
belong. take me to the golden city

by the bay, where the breeze is crisp and hills
rise high enough to touch the sun blessing
the ocean, streets, and cable cars with its
midas touch, the bridge glowing in the fog.

take me there and let me ache for my own
smog-filled city of the angels—my home.

chicano yearn

it's almost ridiculous, this
innate longing we carry
to belong to two places

at once: un poquitito
de aquí, un poquitito
de allá. we're aching

the way our grandparents,
homesick and empty, satisfy
themselves with the *idea*

of their motherland,
strolling olvera street on
the weekends, content

con los recuerditos de
piel, ollas de barro,
marionetas de colores.

we know nothing more
than this—shit, most of us
chicanos have never even *been*

to mexico anyway. all we have
are the stories passed along
at the dinner table

(after we've wiped our plates
clean con tortillas) and routines
we've learned to mimic:

our whispered prayers
to la virgen, gardens of herbs
in the front yard, sweeping

to heartbroken musicians
every sunday the way our mothers
mopped to los angeles azules

singing *¿cómo no acordarme*
de ti? ¿de qué manera olvidarte?
look at how we gravitate

towards passion, falling
in love with everything
at least once—

even these american cities
we come from, imperfect
and inglorious

because we've learned
to take pride in our roots
no matter how broken.

we don't mean to romanticize,
know our neighborhoods
can be dangerous, that most

of us live in crowded apartments
and can't so much as look out
the window at night. but we've

learned happiness must hurt
somehow. laughter aches in the belly,
a smile yanks at the corners of the mouth.

and what are we if not these places
we've grown up in? el mercadito
de east los on the weekends

with our bolsitas de chocomil,
the swap meet on alameda
where mama does back to school

shopping, y los callejones where we'll cry
and cry for one of those tiny turtles
in a plastic tank. we yearn to belong

somewhere undeniably american
and mexican all at once. an echo
of our homes, a place to call our own:

in this country we were born into
but carbon copy of that *other* land
we know.

santa desconocida
—para las inmigrantes who never made it across

serenity
in the eye of the storm.
here lies mi tia,
      my sister,
      mi abuela,
      my cousin,
      myself.

see the moon, pale as a spectre
against the blackening sky. i
do not believe in god

while caught in this cataclysmic
        chaos: the hills silhouetted

on the horizon, all burnt
sienna and umber, the saguaro
growing stiff, surrendering to the night.
the shadows l e n g t h e n i n g

among the vastness of this desert plane,
even as skin begins to bruise, the blood
to settle, the bones to break—*for dust
we are and to dust we shall return.*

santa desconocida, mujer sagrada,
amiga mía, cariño, mi niña,
¿que te hicieron?

venias por tu camino y te desviaron,
te dejaron aquí entre piedra y arena.

an unwritten poem
lingers there at your core,
blooming along the curves
of your frame

as spring bloomed
on the hills of eden,
beyond this borderland.

reach out and whisper it
to the stars slowly
awakening.

tell them what you dreamt of,
tell them what you're dreaming.

the american dreamer awakens

i.

in a 7-eleven parking lot at 6 a.m.,
penny scratching at the lottery ticket.
dreamer is feeling lucky today:

the sunrise is beautiful, car started
no problem, and junior earned
a certificate at school

—for perfect attendance that is,
 pero pues, algo es algo.

dreamer imagines hitting it big,
buying a house in beverly hills.
there'd be a white picket fence,
níspero y guayaba trees

in the front yard, una virgencita
de barro by the walkway, classic
cherry red cadillac in the garage.

ceramic tiles in the kitchen,
no vinyl cover on the couch,
and everyone would have
their very own bedroom:

junior, melissa, angelica,
jose, alex, isabel, él y su señora,
y hasta el perro.

si, dreamer grins.
hasta el firulais también.

ii.

in a 6th grade english class at 10 a.m.,
reading martin luther king jr.'s speech.
little dreamer realizes violence exists

beyond her own block. she's heard
gunshots across the street, helicopters
loud in the middle of the night. seen
blood pooled on the curb

and her local corner market ransacked.
even at the age of 11, she understands
that certain parts of L.A. are "*ghetto*"

meaning *poor*,
meaning *broken.*
now,

history and literature intertwine on her desk.
rosa parks claims her seat on an alabama bus,
the watsons move to birmingham where kenny
learns the correlation between churches and bombs.

m.l.k. has a dream in d.c. and rodney king
is brutally assaulted by the police, enraging
her entire city, which burns, *burns, b u r n s.*

why care? her friend shrugs. *we're not black.*

but anne frank tip-toes up to her attic for hanukkah
and japanese-americans are sent to war to kill
the japanese for the americans

and little dreamer knows being brown
is not that different.

if it happened to them,
it could happen to us.

iii.

in his own bedroom at 2 p.m.,
to the sound of a fist pounding on the door.
                BANG!   *BANG!*   *BANG!*

it has all come to this, dreamer thinks.
those three knocks. they correspond
to the thumping of his heart.

they correspond to the thwack of his hammer,
hitting the nail on the head every time, straining his back
building houses he could never afford.
                    BANG!   *BANG!*   *BANG!*

they correspond to the sound of his boots stomping
on the pavement the day he ran away from home.
he couldn't look back, *wouldn't* look back. el salvador,
his motherland, at war. every night the guns firing
into the air, tearing at the sky. *every night*
                    BANG!   *BANG!*   *BANG!*

somewhere downtown, he heard the people
were protesting. waving their flags and cardboard signs.
taking over the streets, circling city hall. they were flowing
onto the freeways: men, women, children.
even the concheros in their penachos
striking their drums
                    BANG!   *BANG!*   *BANG!*

whatever happened to the american dream,
land of the free, that liberty and justice they speak of?
why are they here, knocking like this, ready to seize him?

all he ever did was work.
all he ever did was want, dream, hope.

my father teaches me to whistle
—for my father and the resplendent quetzal

a serpent-tailed bird perches between my father's teeth,
emerald and iridescent, black-eyed and yellow beaked.
he has plucked this feathered creature from the cloud
forest for me, smuggled it across borders

between his lips: a piece of the motherland,
kukulkan's spirit, quetzalcoatl's being. i inherit
a part of the bird like a mayan monarch, no crown
of long green plumage but a song, strange

on an american city street, sad without the giant oaks
dripping beneath the white white clouds. it is years
before i hear of how the quetzal ceased singing
when the spanish invaded, locked shackles

on the ankles, the wrists, tossed the mayan gods back
to the stars. i am only five, too young to question the bird's
belly dyed red in tecún umán's blood, chichen itza left to rot,
my father's nightmares of a war in his heart. i simply do as he does:

tuck tongue behind teeth and pucker my lips,
as if to kiss the breeze. let loose the song of gentle winds
underwing, guatemalan mountaintops beckoning. let loose
the sound of heaven and earth, of ancestral sorrow
buried deep in the marrow, the bone.

middle

i think of us often. epitome of youth in the foreground of a gas station, clustered at the bus stop: this was our place. we'd cling to childhoods spent playing make-believe, this here our last game, this here the last place we played pretend. we thought we were women even though we hadn't reached adulthood quite yet. a single body of individuals all clumsy-limbed, baby-faced, clad in school uniforms; disheveled. wild bodies moving to the rhythm of shadows dancing in our hands, golden hour approaching. sunlight filtered through the tree leaves above us; clouds decorated our heads. we were loud enough to drown out the city, lights & sounds a blur around us. ocean waves around rocks rooted amidst the tumble, trying to chisel us to sand.

we'd pull petals off of the wildflowers as a means to ease hearts aching after the boys avoided us in the halls, ignored the blushing, tenderhearted joy of our 'i like you's' shouted across streets, first sparks of love burnt out cold, nothing but smoke—boys always kill the prettiest things. even the sun wished to leave, changing the color of the clouds like a countdown. the traffic light blinking us closer to the sidewalk's end. still, we scattered ampersands like dice on the dirt floor & braided semicolons into our sentences because we refused to part ways. the bus would come, we'd always wait for the next. deep in our subconscious, we knew we were like dandelions—once we came undone, we'd never come together again.

it's quiet here now;
nothing but tree leaves learning
to scatter in wind.

our neighborhood's gone bad

they've done it again, have manifested their destiny /   across our slanted roofs and
      rusted pipes. /   i hardly recognize this place anymore, /   even the shadows
dance askant, elongating past /   unfamiliar buildings, sleek and cavernous, all sharp/
                    edges and concrete walls. look, *el payasito* /   party supplies
is gone. las piñatas that once hung /   outside on the chain link fence, papel picado
      bleaching /   in the sun—cardboard spiderman next to la chilindrina /   next to a funny
looking minnie mouse—have vanished. /   in its stead, they've made an
art gallery where someone's /   hung up trash they picked up off the streets, /
      call it *urban decay*, groundbreaking, *deep.* /   that empty lot mr. benny used to
      keep his chickens in /   is for sale, covered in blue plastic tarp. beside it, /   los gringos
      have opened up yet *another* cafe there, /   where la señora gonzalez had her restaurant. you
      know, /   where las viejitas loved to congregate after church, /   devouring
their tortas de tamale, passing around /   the latest gossip like salt? yeah, that
      one. and look, /   remember the cisneros' house with the citrus trees /   that would
poke over the garden wall? /   the ones we used to steal those oranges from /
on our way to school, pockets weighed down /   with the contraband fruit? it's all right there,
      /   where the cars are now parked /   in their neat little spaces, right atop / where the
      kitchen used to be, the living room, / the garage. can you see the ghost /   of our neighborhood
still /   lingering here, holding on? /   it's there, i can feel it, like an ache /
in the chest, a sour taste in my mouth. /   how do we lay it to rest? can we /
bring it back to life? i find myself /   nearly walking into walls sometimes, /
      my own feet following paths that no longer exist, /   don't lead anywhere at all. soon,
only you and i will be left /   to remember what this place once was /   and even then,
that memory will fade and warp, /   until someone comes and says *this used to be an ugly slum /
      'til we made it better, we made it safe.* / will we believe him then, / their reality
            filling in the gaps/   we left on the street /   and in our hearts?

somewhere on mulholland drive

you're losing it:
heartbeat palpable
from where i am

sitting, your hands
shaking. you breathe
deep to steady nerves

pulsing like seismic
waves. i only watch.

i never thought i
could cause this
in a man.

the night is lovely.
darkness hums, cold
air blows sharply

against the glass
of my window,
i like this place

you've brought me
to. the city stretched out
at my feet, the sky wide

and inviting.
last time i was kissed,
it had been silly

and soft. childish.
the thought of you
excites me. you say

my eyes make you want
to give me the world.
you grin, dumb

with feeling.
imagining forever.
but then,

when you lean in,
that's when it begins

—hand on my thigh,
tongue on my lips,
the clock soft,

going
tick
tick
tick.

my situationship thinks he's better than me

cause his spanish is better than mine.
cause he's from the hood.
cause su familia owns land back in mexico.
cause he's actually *been* to mexico.
cause he listened to bad bunny before he got big.
cause he's street smart.
cause he can drive with one hand.
cause he called his ex a *bitch*.
cause he hates his dad.

i know un machista when i see one,
big wannabe tough guy who thinks
with the thing between his legs.

but i'm stupid and lonely
and we're here, parked
by the side of the road,
dangerously close

to the precipice.
if i opened my door
i'd fall over the edge.

and maybe i like it,
this rush of adrenaline.
here is the type of man
i've always been warned
against.

and he's holding me
and kissing me
and our skin
is awash in
moonlight.

and isn't this what love is supposed to be like
—laying yourself out on the chopping block,
hoping for tenderness in the knife?

tectonic

i was born   between tectonic plates, right at the wound that moves
earthquake-like: as chaotic as its people, as confused as those
tremors seized   canyons & valleys split by the earth,
my mother who ruptured, a   spasmodic stretching of soil, of souls,
tsunami of tears   here, we all carry a bit of the quake
dry in the throat,   a cataclysmic urge to ruin all, even our own
body in bloom   here we are metamorphic
& i emerging   shifting with each tick of the clock,
a genetic map of   people with hollow hands that grip for ghosts, we're
fault lines in constant motion,   intertwined, lost within
shifting between   dreamscapes that leave us hungry & realities too close to
the unstable, ever on the brink of   those fissures along our hearts forged by
a self-destruction   a seismic yearning to mimic our
all too familiar   home, the hills & ravines
to the mountains eroding on the coasts   forced apart by time,
& a violence reserved for the   evolution of soil alive, & the erratic
crashing ocean   tides that remind us we belong to the land

malibu, ca

indigo;
white cascading off
of the crest of a wave.

mama fishes
for pretty rocks to hold
against the swell
of her belly.

she knows tenderness here
is momentary, quick
as a blink of an eye. water
caresses the beach
before striking

and splattering against it
and everything shatters—
even the mountains crumble
under the tide.

but mama pretends
she is a lighthouse. she stands
in the sand and watches
a hermit crab discard its shell
at her feet, little sailor
abandoning ship.

the shell, perfect spiral,
entices her. its edges broken,
the white speckled as brown as earth.
how nice it'd be to cocoon oneself
into its folds.

mama presses an ear to its cavity.
the water whispers against the nacre
like the rush of blood,
crimson tinged cobalt.

it is her heart
and the ocean's breath
in her eardrums.

somewhere within her womb,
the child shifts. soon, mama thinks,
her own body will be hollow too,
her bones echoing memories.

she'll cut her thumb
on the edge of a knife or bite
her tongue years from now,
recall the child's foot
against her ribs

and the empty shell
on the sand at her feet,
know that no pain can
compare to this:
of her child

growing,
growing,
gone.

no. 61
—for d.v.

side by side
before a rothko:
rust and blue.

you
do not understand
the concept of color
without structure.

i
explain
that canvases can
sometimes be mirrors.
      caught between
          these shades,

we are
standing

       at the crosswalk   in the summer,
       worlds sprouting from our tongues
           as the sun
                 burns us red.

                     i tell you of aztec pyramids
                     and the myths i inherited,

             you tell me about summers
             in india and of the universe
                 appearing within

                     the mouth of a god
                       you praise.

we are
dancing

       in the rain   on that day
           we believed ourselves rebellious,

        walking out   with our eyes
          turned up
              towards all that gray,   everyone staring,
    wondering if
         the droplets
      on our lashes came
                 from the clouds or the sadness
                      we'd been
                   drowning in.

we are
running

    down the streets   in the evening
       as the night bruises   the sidewalks blue. you
             and i chasing after the bus,
        the air in our ears   as sharp as our mothers' tongues
        while we laugh up at the moon like wolves.

we are
holding

    our breath   in the dark,
       your confessions rising like bubbles   and exploding like bombs.
        if life is like a road, you say,
           then can we choose when to   stop?
      that you're tired   after sprinting through youth
        and   to keep on living seems like such a long walk.

we are
drifting

    as we age. the clock   naturally   pulling   us   apart
      as if we were sitting on the teeth
          of two   different   cogs   spinning
in opposite   directions,
      attempting
        to understand   ourselves and each other.

    side   by   side

within this painting,

you
eager to move on
to the next artwork
on the wall,

i
still trying to tell you
how rare it is, our kind
of love.

mnemonic

what if our body knew of the land it would call home, held a map of the place it came from,
long before we inhabited it? i'd like to have been born with my city in the palm, main–
taining it close. lines like sidewalks, highways, and alleys. pads of the fingers mountains, spring
blooming eternal: bougainvillea, sage, california poppies. trace the blue and green veins down to
the wrist. here, the L.A. river hums, dreaming of its buried river bed. follow broadway,

wedged between skin and bone, in all its former glory—movie palaces glowing and
streetcars gliding smooth down roads. on that scar beneath forefinger (healed over
a week ago) runs angels flight, tugging gently up the slope: think opening day, 1901. the
valleys and knolls, rising and falling. rich folks climbing up bunker hill
where their victorian mansions stand guard. soon the land will sell, homes turned to
apartments for rent, hotels; broken to bits for families of five, of nine. bright olive–

green fields thriving along the flesh: oranges and persimmons, lemons and grapes. oh!
to go back to the days before this was all tamed under concrete and asphalt. what i wouldn't
give to see sheep and cattle grazing in the pastures again. a spring gurgling downhill, its
waters sweet, sparkling; naive to the library that would someday be
built atop the path it carved, settled on the soil and stones. city hall, tall and grand,

would stand at the tip of my thumb overlooking olvera street, union station, chinatown. if
we follow the curve of muscle just above the joint, past the old plaza church, we'd
find all 4 moreton bay figs alive again. their canopy of green proving anything foreign could
thrive on angeleno soil: its roots burrowed within the earth. my city of hope,
of dreams, a history buried deep, fossilized within the pavement. i'd want to

hold everything it ever was—the forgotten flora and fauna, the broken brick and mortar. i'd pick
a line from my palm, play fortune teller. read all the land remembers; ridges in skin like braille, a
story transcending space and time. i'd hold it out, fingers extended like petals of a flower
in bloom: cars inching down freeways, palm trees swaying on street corners crowded, people on
the move. sun setting on the horizon, glowing golden through my city, flowing down figueroa.

city hall, 26th floor

mama remembers climbing
guava trees as a little girl.

skirt tied around her waist,
knobby knees bruised, skin red
down to the ankles. tree trunks
rough against her calves

and soles of her feet. she reaches
out for the next twisted branch,
fruit ripe and sticky, sweet
juice dripping, beautifully

green against the clouds.
she looks down from her perch,
a bird watching over the earth,

     infinite.

         i am on top of the world
        within my steel and concrete tree,

         the entire city in miniature.
       from up here, i remember mama's
     stories, wonder what she'd have thought
          of this at 12 years-old.

            wish
         i could bring her here,
       show her this, give her more
          than guavas ripe
         on the tip of a branch;

          offer her the life
       she fought to bestow on me
       and nurture the child she was.

PED XING

palm

first tree i could name.
those upside down brooms, sweeping
up the sun, stars, moon.

migrant plant, rooted
deep beneath my feet. where else
could you grow but here?

leaves like fireworks
exploding high above my
man-made oasis.

la llorona at the border

woman weeps
by the river's edge,
her hands like hooks
in rippling water, fishing

out a shoe tiny
as a mollusk's shell.
she only meant to cross over
to the other side. paradise

hovered there—mirage
in the desert. but the river
slithered, sunk its teeth
into the child cradled

in her arms. another one
gone. now the woman
wanders by the river's edge,
frigid water pulsating

like a million hearts.
she'll wander forever
if she must, for the river
showed no mercy

but a mother's love
knows no bounds.

the flower vendor

i've seen her a hundred times,
 shouldering flora like a mountain
carries spring on its back. she sits
under sunlight pouring love

into calla lilies's tongues trumpeting
for summer's end. her bandaged hands
bleed where the flesh gives way
to thorns and the sharp filaments

of broken stems and cellophane.
she holds her basket like an offering
to the cars driving by from the side
of the road. roses radiant against concrete,

their shadows stretching into darkness
as daylight turns to dusk—not
a single blossom sold. yet she dreams
of flowers on skin brown as earth,

growing down her spine, anchoring
themselves along the grooves
in her bones, they correspond. beauty
overflows. she sits at the root,

shouldering it all
strong and unyielding,
waiting for the sun.

no sabo[1]
—*after jenn givhan*

i'm losing[2] my spanish,
stumbling over words
i could easily cry out
before the age of five.

es que se me olvida[3];
mi color *azul* loses its zest,
turns *blue* y el *corazon*
skips a beat, turns *heart*.

i stutter and stop, blushing
at the stiff and awkward
consonants and vowels
escaping my mouth[4]. i can't

even roll my *r*'s smooth
as a machine gun[5]. i wonder,
as the words crack and break
between my teeth, spilling out

in fragments[6], is this how it was
when my ancestors[7] lost the war
against foreign tongues, spanish
forced unto them, their world

1. we giggle and mock anyone who can't speak good 'til that wannabe white, cara de nopal latina "blonde" with the brown roots scoffs and sneers at us for being too brown. nothings funny after that.
2. people are forsaking their culture, their roots,
3. letting it fade like a birthmark: slowly, slowly, and then all at once.
4. sometimes i look in the mirror to see if i can trace my ancestry: take in the shape of my teeth, shade of my lips, curve of the jaw.
5. i wonder what else, besides language, did i inherit through violence?
6. i cling to any little thing i can: tortillas hechas a mano, mi medallita de la virgen, the chiquihuite in the kitchen, red string around the wrist.
7. i want to be the one that remembers, holds everything my family taught me, keeps it close.

destroyed[8] and rebuilt anew
all in a different light? were they
laughed at too, for borrowing
and braiding their nahuatl roots[9]

into the spaniard's vocabulary?
no hay que achicopalarse. ven aquí,
te quiero apapachar. i practice
the art of preservation

speaking in spanglish[10] when
the words mama taught me
just aren't enough. everything
is working in tandem

attempting to erase my heritage,
my history. i don't want to lose
myself in translation, forget
where i come from, where i belong.

8. our history is being swept under a rug, our own people forgetting where they come from,
   who they are.
9. i want to stay rooted, remember, be proud.
10. walk out with ribbons in my braids, nopal en la frente and claim, "soy mexicana, pero
    americana tambien—like it or not."

you hate L.A. traffic
—for n.j.r

we're caught between a tow truck and a semi, stuck on the 110, beneath a bridge

defend this? the dodgers just lost and we're stuck amongst the cars trickling like

honey,

going nowhere slowly. hundreds of rubber tires grind against this asphalt

stadium. *that was.* every angelino knows *that* story, the little mexican-american barrio

turned

cautionary tale. but before that this was all green pasture, mustard blooming under

we're inching along on a modern road, congested and unhappy. *but no, yeah.* i say.

the

stadium sits atop palo verde, la loma, bishop; atop houses, a school, and a church

the skyscrapers and the parking lots and the highways that everyone here hates driving

on.

it's hard to believe but before there was us, there were farmlands. before that, *trees*

planning, you say. but this is capitalism at its finest, the *city planning* to make it

big.

when money talks, the city listens to anything but the earth, the people and

44

someone's painted dodger blue. *this is hell*, you say, seething while the hills darken

and you declare how much you hate this city i hold so dear -- but how can i

poultice, our weight rubbing down on the wound buried beneath: the "what once was" but

now isn't. *wasn't this the chavez ravine?* you ask. *no*, i point out the window at the

bees' wings, prickly pear cacti pretty in their red pear crowns. the tongva spent hundreds

of years gathering on this high ground to escape from floods   and now

bulldozed and flattened clean. and that's just *here*. imagine what other stories los viejitos

remember, all the families displaced, gardens dug up, houses torn down for

and *bogs* and *wetlands*. we've paved over the earth and the poor-man's home in the name

of "modernity," meaning "heavy traffic" and "road rage." *this is just poor city*

what they need.

late night drive home
—for p.y.

streetlights flicker white on every other block, illuminating
the planes of your face, bright black of your eyes. we drive
with the windows down, kevin kaarl singing *toda esta ciudad.*
this is all that matters to us: the hollywood hills unraveling,

giving way to highland, sunset, santa monica. we can not stop
laughing, our fingers greasy from the drive-thru burgers and fries,
stories spilling along with the sugar and salt, something sweet
to top it off. we lay out our entire lives in the front seat of your car:

how often we felt alone growing up, depth of our mexican roots,
the lovers who left, fathers who never understood, burdens
our mothers never wanted to pass down to us. we hold
our breath through the tunnels, your blown out speakers

squeaking out morrissey, ivan cornejo, frank ocean, surely tempo;
the music's reverb making your windows rattle. rather than
head straight home, we park by the side of the road and spill
the tea, debrief, announce what we've been thinking of,

yapping like there's no tomorrow. remember that night you drove
me heartbroken and sobbing because a potential lover had gone
all wrong? or when we sat in some parking lot, amazed
by the way an ex-friend refused to grow up? it was an accident

first time we got on the freeway. no driver's license, our palms
slick with sweat, driving with two hands on the steering wheel. you
were afraid of us crashing, rear door smashed, shards of glass
everywhere. i kept my faith, lost no hope, believed you'd get us *somewhere*

safely. as our exit whizzes by and you're remembering everything
you ever learned about how to safely merge, i wonder where we'd
end up if we keep going. you and i arriving at some desert, mountain,
a town close to the coast—never looking back so long as there's a road.

streetlights flicker white on every other block. **i**lluminating
the planes of your face, bright b**l**ack **o**f your eyes. we dro**ve**
with the windows down, kevin kaarl singing toda esta ciudad.
this was all that mattered to us: the holl**y**wo**o**d hills **u**nraveling,

giving way to h**igh**land, **s**unset, santa monica. we can **not** stop
laughing, our fingers greasy from the drive-thru burgers and fries,
stories spilling along with the sugar and salt. **something swe**et
to top it off. we lay out our entire lives in the front **s**e**a**t of **y**our car

how **often** we felt alone **growing up**. depth of our **mexican** roots,
the **love**rs who left, fathers who never understood. burdens
our mothers never **w**anted to p**as**s down to us. we hold
our breath through the tunnels, your blown out speakers

squeaking out **mor**rissey, ivan cornejo, fr**a**nk oce**a**n, surely tempo.
the music's re**verb** making your windows rattle. rather **than**
head str**a**ight home, we park by the side of the road and spill
the tea, debrief, an**noun**ce what we've been thinking of,

yapping like there's no tomorrow. remember that night **you** drove
me heartbroken and sobbing because a potential **love**r had gone
all wrong? or when we sat in so**me** parking lot, amazed
by the way an ex-friend refused to grow up? it was an accident

first time we got on the freeway, no driver's license, our palms
slick with sweat. **driving** with two hands on the steering wheel, you
were afraid of **us** crashing, rear door smashed, shards of glass
everywhere. **i** kept my faith, **lo**st no hope, belie**ve**d **you**'d get us somewhere

safely, as our exit whizzes **by** and you're **remembering everything**
you ever learned about how to safely merge. I **w**ond**e**r **w**h**ere** we'd
end up if we **keep** go**ing you** and I arriving at some desert. mountain,
a town **close** to the coast —never looking back, so long as there's a road

a rorschach on the moon

this is   is this
the time   time the
of saturnine memory,   memory saturnine? of
driving down winding roads, solitary.   solitary roads, winding down, driving.
only your face   face your only
within the moon   moon. the within
chasing me.   me chasing
you   you—
coveted the goodbye, no   no goodbye. the coveted
care for wounds inflicted. ruthless &   & ruthless inflicted wounds, for care
lonely, i long for, not pain…oh, need i   i need, oh pain, not for long. i? lonely,
tell you?   you tell
heart to hand, let me   me, let hand to heart
go back to the best of you, of us.
when you kissed me, i formed a gravitational attachment. when you kissed me
i decided you'd   become the world,   you'd decided i
be   the brightest thing in the night sky.   be
moonlight on cold pavement, as white as bridal dress & the foam of ocean waves.
you keep leaving
even when   when even
i try to drive to you
i fear that soon   soon that fear i
dawn will erupt   erupt will dawn
the road will end
& what of us?   us of what? &
you'll fall, dragging my love   love, my dragging fall, you'll
past the horizon, somewhere   somewhere horizon, the past
i cannot follow.   follow not, can i?
is this us ending?   ending us this is.
another day another love but   but love, another day another
always you, you, you   you, you, you always
accompanying the night: night the accompanying
unreachable.   unreachable.

angeleno sunsets remind me of you

the women in my family have learned that love
consumes flesh like wax until the soul dies out
—wick of a candle in smoke. they say it hurts

most of the time. that love, like a sunset
can be incandescent for a second, then darkness
in ash. *a woman's place is within fire, you need*

to burn to feel alive. and yet, my love has blued,
become something i can dive into; blue moon
on the radio, blue nude on a wall. i have learned
that love should not combust, batter and bruise,

be red as a wound. it should be me holding you
in my arms, the world tilting underfoot and the sky
swaddling us whole, burying us deep
between the clouds.

ghazal for westlake/macarthur park

do you remember what it was like to be free there, in the dark?
before they caged you up like a wild beast, there, in the dark?

you were glorious once: slick with mud and swollen after the rains
replenished your oasis. you'd stretch out to breathe there, in the dark,

across the acres and acres you claimed as your own. your water lapping
on your shores like hands taking all it could cease, there in the dark.

only in the summer would you hide, burrow back into the silt
and clay, let the soil swallow you in the heat there, in the dark.

it was the men who broke and shrunk you, tamed your wild, wild ways.
your swamp became a lake, your soul static under concrete there, in the dark.

i've seen the black and white photographs of you, now yellowed
and faded: the forgotten boathouse, the lake, the trees, there in the dark.

in my own memory, your streets speak to me in my mother tongue:
todo el mundo me quiere arreglar o alimentar aquí en la oscuridad.

las señoras sell pupusas y tamales at the metro station; cobblers, doctors,
and repairmen set up shop, hoping to mend, cure, relieve there in the dark.

chain link fences line your sidewalks now. you've been deemed dangerous,
helpless, rotten beneath the homeless and the seagull's feet, there in the dark.

you attract the broken, clinging to them, hoping for a way out. if i hold my breath,
i can hear your swamp waters sussuring, still alive beneath me, there in the dark.

las viejitas on the metro a-line want to be immortal

 the world is crumbling
outside my window;

houses give way to strip malls,
give way to parking structures,
give way to empty lots.

everything collapses
then rises once more
in an endless loop, flat
against the glass. time

plows through everything,
as callous as this train which cuts
across the hills, the valleys,
the freeways, someone's backyard.

passersby fade. flowers bloom, wither,
and fall in the span of a second like eyes
opening, widening, then closing shut.

 we come to a stop.

three old women detach themselves
from this armageddon, boarding the train
like gusts of wind: boisterous and riveting.

fíjese que cuando yo era niña,
quería ser actriz...

> *¡no me diga! yo soñaba con*
> *vivir aquí, en el extranjero.*

 ...actriz como maria félix.

> *yo solo pensaba en sobrevivir.*

they lay out their entire lives
across the aisle, wear their hearts
stitched to the front of their sweaters,
bundled up thick in spite of the heat.

time is taking down everything
in its path out there: mountains fall,
cars rot on street corners, abandoned
buildings stew in their stillness.
nothing is built to last.

pero las viejitas pull us all
into their orbit. they've got
the whole train listening.

> *quería ser diseñadora de ropa.*
> *quería abrir mi propia tienda…*

> *¡tenía un novio bien guapo,*
> *me dijo que yo sería estrella!*

> *pasabamos hambre,*
> *y solo teníamos frijol y maíz.*

the men, women, and children
exiting, glance back at them
and their puckered lips, graying
hair, twinkling eyes.

> *vine aquí de niña para poder*
> *mandarle dinero a mi familia.*

> *tuve una hija y pues, paré de soñar.*

> *la tienda… nunca la abrí.*

i reach the end of the line.
the train doors open and remain
open to the relentless ticking
of the clock outside.

las viejitas me miran, sonrien.

> *yo era alguien, tuve sueños.*

> *tu eresjoven,mija.*
> *tienes tiempo.*

> *recuerda, cuando tengas mi*
> *edad, sabrás lo que te quiero decir.*

slowly, they hobble out, continuing
their narratives past the train station
and around the block, autochorous

as the oak, cementing their roots
deep. i watch as they fade away
into the void, living forever
in my memory.

oldiez
—for k.c.

we want the kind of love they sing about in oldiez songs.
that real, king cole type of l - o - v - e spilling out

the lowriders cruising down the street. we desire *only you,
earth angel.* something fancy and classy like the pachucos

in their zoot suits and fedoras, with the feathers down to here.
we yearn for something permanent like the homies who've got

their lovers inked beautiful right on the jugular, zigzagging
across the veins. we want love to bleed in our names. give us

the kind that bring us pura serenata. mariachi in moonlight
like chente, negrete, infante in those black and white movies

mama watches on tv. we want the passionate, telenovela type
that sing boleros out our windows, *sin ti es inútil vivir…*

give us the good stuff. the yearning, til-death, tug of the heart
strings. that love that inspires las señoras to sing along

to k-love on the radio as they sweep, their brooms
like metronomes. selena blasting from someone's stereo,

i just wanna hold you close. we've lived too long wishing
and wanting what every love song has promised:

an escape from the loneliness, the limerence, the bad luck.
we want to ease that ache in the chest, hear someone say

we belong together for eternity. un amor que no muere,
something real, something true. loud as trompetas

and as pure as the white white clouds
floating in an east l.a. summer sky.

we walk through angelino heights
—for n.j.r.

crickets chirp from the flower beds, serenading the orchids and the lilac
rustling in the dark. my love of you overflows in this stillness, as the world
shuts its eyes and finally succumbs to the quiet, everything nestled comfortably

against the night. you and i are the only two here, footsteps rhythmic
on pavement. we are searching for the oldest house on the block
in this hundred-year-old neighborhood, pointing at turrets and towers,

hand-carved wooden railings, and stained glass windows. it fascinates me,
this preservation of luxury. soon, i'll rant about the way black and brown
communities are demolished everyday, stripped of their little bit of earth.

but for now, let me bask in the beauty of these homes, holding their breath,
the ancient trees rubbing their branches against the stars. let us play our game
of choosing which of these we want: the pale, pale yellow from the *thriller*

music video or the sea foam green with the white shutters, the one that reminds
us both of san francisco. let us pretend we're already married and can afford one
of these victorian mansions frozen in time. i've never lived in a proper house before,

with a yard all to myself and a room of my own. we speak a little lower, planning
the home we'll someday build: resilient, beautiful, set atop a sturdy foundation.
something like what we already have, you and i, walking hand in hand.

what i know about "el lay"
—*after sarah borjas*

(3)
                              rots, remains forgotten. i know
this is where they'll bury me, under the power lines
stitching the sky, quilt-like. my bones, my blood,
\my skin mingling with the dirt beneath the trash,
the shoes, broken lamps, shattered glass by the side
of the road, joining the desiccated river beds,
mummified roots, those relinquished ancestors.
the discarded

(5)
                              grip at the soil
the way the tree roots do, bursting gnarled fingers through
the concrete, reclaiming what's been entombed. sembrando
raíces amongst chickens and dogs, under the insects,
under the muck. the nopales, mangos, naranjas, y caña
that grow through chain link fences, beyond borders

(2)
                              asking the saints
for salvation every sunday, devout as priests, recite
their holy prayers within their cavernous churches:
virgen santísima de guadalupe, reina de los ángeles,
ruega por nosotros y nuestras familias... i know
the historic sites, the landmarks, & victorian mansions
derelict within an immigrant's neighborhood which

(4)
                              rise again,
made anew from the ashes because this is a place
where things never truly die. full of latinos & immigrants
who can't *ever* seem to throw away *anything*—the theaters
turned swap meets in downtown & westlake a testament
to this. i know los viejitos who burrow in their gardens and

59

(9)

                    call it *the entire world.*
the ocean crashing along the dunes, caressing
this corner of the universe, san gabriel mountains
along the horizon like sleeping giants resting at the edge
of this great basin, filled to the brim with dreamers,
a bit of ourselves forever a part of this ground
humming beneath our soles.

(6)

                    like a beacon of hope
which feed hungry passersby on their way through life.
those color wheel sombrillas staked at the curb mean sliced
fruta con limón, elotes y esquites, el señor de los raspados
scraping away at the ice block. everything handed to us
tenderly cradled in the palm which is how i learned love
is supposed to be offered despite

(1)

                    this intrinsic chaos we carry
originating from somewhere deep, rooted in the tectonic
plates brutally grinding against each other; the cars
smashing & splintering at the junction; pigeons
beating at the wind. we are always on edge here,
ready to burn, riot, break, bleed. i know the old
women that clutch at their rosaries

(8)

                    becoming one
magnificent dreamscape. the way that spanglish here
gives way to konglish gives way to singlish gives way
to linguistic hybrids yet unheard of —a mosaic of languages
plastered on billboards and the sides of buildings
because we yearn to be heard, to be understood, to belong.
i know the tongva believe these mountains, hills & valleys
sacred, call it tovaangar,

(7)
                            my aching heart. i know
the names, pawprints, dates, the love letters etched
into wet cement & left to dry are what will remain
when time sweeps up everything else, smooth as a tidal
wave. the music pouring out of windows, history
immortalized through murals on walls, that graffiti
inscribed at bus stops, overpasses, unfinished
skyscrapers, all that defines this place
when i think of where i come from

homecoming

the bus rumbles ever onward & you wonder why
i'd never leave here, emphasizing the ghostly world hidden in smog. you'd do
anything to desert these streets unraveling like ribbons in windows. but love,
i am rooted here, as deep as the very palm trees swaying, always hoping &
praying for better days, not a better place. the blue sky bruises black & i'd hate
to live away from the skyscrapers scattered like dice along the coast, the sound
of ocean so close to the clogged up veins of freeways strained, people just
taking up space, wishing on the stars that someone has paved the
sidewalks with. here, both night & day feel and fade in the same
way: too slow and yet, scampering quickly as if afraid to stay. still, to
love its flaws is to love L.A.—at least that's what love means to me.

notes

"santa desconocida" is an ekphrastic poem inspired by Judithe Hernandez's painting of the same name, viewed at The Cheech Marin Center for Chicano Art & Culture of the Riverside Art Museum.

"no sabo[1]" was inspired by Jenn Givhan's poem "Endtimes Meditation on Mothering Self-Care[1]."

"mnemonic" is a golden shovel after the mnemonic device used to memorize the Downtown L.A. streets. The original creator of this mnemonic device remains unknown.

The line, "we want the kind of love they sing about in oldiez songs" takes after a line written by Sara Borjas. *"only you"* is a reference to the song "Only You, And You Alone" by The Platters. "earth angel" references the song "Earth Angel" by Marvin Berry & The Starlighters. *"sin ti es inútil vivir..."* is a lyric from "Sin Ti" by Los Panchos. *"i just wanna hold you close"* is a lyric from "Dreaming of You" by Selena. *"we belong together for eternity"* is a lyric from "We Belong Together" by Ritchie Valens.

"what i know about 'el lay'" is after Sara Borjas' "What I Know About Fresno."

"homecoming" is a golden shovel that borrows a line from the song "seoul" by RM.

acknowledgements

I would like to thank the following publications for first publishing these poems:

> "middle" appeared in *wind-up mice press*' "Sunday Nibbles"
> "tectonic" appeared in the *Exposition Review*
> "malibu, ca" appeared in *orangepeel mag.*

This book would not be possible without my mother's unyielding support. Since the moment I learned to read, she never stopped buying me books. ¡Muchas gracias, Mami!

Thank you to Disha, my childhood best friend who spent several years walking through Downtown L.A. with me, philosophizing on everything. Those conversations really helped shape my outlook on life. Thank you for always supporting me!

To Paulina—your love and friendship mean so much to me! I appreciate you for always driving us everywhere every time we explored the city.

To Noah, who teaches me patience and perseverance every single day. Those days on the couch, watching you play *Dark Souls* while I worked on my manuscript helped me more than you know. I love you forever, I promise!

Thank you so much to my *La Poeta Publication* co-ambassadors: Salma Alejo, Chelsea Patricia Ramirez, and Melina Lovera. Your work-ethic, poems, and kind words during our workshops encouraged me and kept me writing.

Thank you forever to the team behind *La Poeta Publications* Kelsey and Joan; both of you put as much work as I did in making my book a reality.

And special thanks to the owner and founder of *La Poeta Publications*, my mentor Celeste Alyssa Gomez—you are such an inspiration to me. Thank you so much for your time, your kind words, and your encouragement. This book would have probably never seen the light of day if you had not selected me for the program and pushed me to keep writing. Thank you, thank you, thank you!

about the author

Alejandra Medina is a Chicana writer from Los Angeles, California. A two time Best of the Net nominee, her work has appeared in multiple publications, most notably *Exposition Review, Breadfruit. Magazine*, and *LatinaMedia.Co*. She currently contributes to *The Luna Collective* as a music journalist. This is her debut poetry chapbook.

Follow Alejandra on Instagram
@amedina.a